T0208550

THE
AWAKENED
LIFE

UMA ALEXANDRA BEEPAT

BALBOA.
PRESS

A DIVISION OF HAY HOUSE

This book is a work of non-fiction. Unless otherwise noted, the author and the publisher
make no explicit guarantees as to the accuracy of the information contained in this book
and in some cases, names of people and places have been altered to protect their privacy.

For more information on Uma Alexandra Beepat, Lotus
Wellness Center, or The Awakened Life, visit:
www.lotuswellnesscenter.net
www.umalotusflower.com

Balboa Press books may be ordered through booksellers or by contacting:

Balboa Press
A Division of Hay House
1663 Liberty Drive
Bloomington, IN 47403
www.balboapress.com
1 (877) 407-4847

Because of the dynamic nature of the Internet, any web addresses or links contained in
this book may have changed since publication and may no longer be valid. The views
expressed in this work are solely those of the author and do not necessarily reflect the
views of the publisher, and the publisher hereby disclaims any responsibility for them.

The author of this book does not dispense medical advice or prescribe the use of any
technique as a form of treatment for physical, emotional, or medical problems without the
advice of a physician, either directly or indirectly. The intent of the author is only to offer
information of a general nature to help you in your quest for emotional and spiritual well-
being. In the event you use any of the information in this book for yourself, which is your
constitutional right, the author and the publisher assume no responsibility for your actions.

Print information available on the last page.

ISBN: 978-1-9822-0659-8 (sc)
ISBN: 978-1-9822-0663-5 (e)

Library of Congress Control Number: 2018907032

Balboa Press rev. date: 06/22/2018

DEDICATION

This book is dedicated to my children Nathaniel and Joshua who awakened me to Life, to my partner Rob who awakened me to Love and to my clients and students who awakened me to my Calling.

Acknowledgements

Thank you to Melissa Schroeder for my foreword and Shelton Fox for her countless hours of editing and believing in me.

Thank you to my mentors and teachers who have personally guided me on this path and taken me further than I could have ever gone on my own.

CONTENTS

FOREWORD

Several years ago, I was in a bad way. Pain had become an everyday occurrence for me and muscle relaxers were my best friends. I suffer from a damage disc in my back that gives me all kinds of trouble. As an author who spends hours in front of the computer, it was starting to damage my career. Massage had helped, but I couldn't find a therapist I liked. The day came when the pain was almost unbearable. In desperation, I got on the Internet and searched. I know now that angels were there to guide me that night. I stumbled upon Uma's website. Little did I know how much my life would change with that decision.

From the first session, I knew I had picked the right person. Healing is second nature to her, as natural as breathing is to everyone else. I found myself feeling better from our first session. Still there was more to come and it affected my life in ways I didn't expect. Uma understands the connection between physical, mental and spiritual illness. Bad energy in one aspect in your life will throw everything off track. During our sessions, I learned of Reiki, of accepting those things I could change and accepting that life doesn't always turn out the way you plan, but it is the way it should turn out.

As I read through Uma's book, so much of what she wrote I remembered from conversations we had. From the very first visit she has guided me to a more open life, allowing me to see the possibilities if I only believe. She has compiled these life lessons in written form, but it is so much more than that. Each section can help you better understand where you need to be on all three of those levels. Each chapter guides you through the steps **you** need to free yourself of the barriers we build that hold us back. I can think of no one else who has more insight or understanding to help you with your quest to a more fulfilling and successful life.

Melissa Schroeder
USA Today Bestselling Author

INTRODUCTION

Namaste. If you live outside the Washington D.C or Northern Virginia area and are not a part of my circle, you probably do not know me or of me. You are probably wondering who I am and what I have to say about this topic that somehow pertains to you.

Let's agree that it *does* pertain to you for the simple reason that the title spoke to you. You have recently undergone or are going through some major life changes. More importantly, you are beginning to see things differently and have a different view on life. In the metaphysical community, we would say you are having an ***awakening***. Depending on whom you talk to, that can mean several different things.

When I first started teaching Reiki in 2009, I used the first *Matrix* movie as an analogy for awakening. That scene where Neo sits across from Morpheus and he has to choose the red pill or the blue pill?

Neo leans in as Morpheus revealed the truth in a deep, deliberate voice – no one can be told what the Matrix is, people have to see it for themselves. In Morpheus's left hand is a blue pill that would allow Neo to remain in blissful ignorance. His right hand holds a red pill that would allow Neo to understand how deep the rabbit hole actually is.

Without all the drama of the *Matrix*, an awakening is similar. *This world is not what you think it is. Life is not what you thought it was.*

What if I told you that many ancient and modern philosophers and gurus have all given the same information about what this experience is all about? Over time we have blindly gone on, ignoring their advice and looking for something different — something more complex to explain it all. That is where *The Awakened Life* comes in — to answer what *it* really is.

Truth is, everyone is awakening and experiencing the same things to varying degrees. However, what is commonly experienced by those awakening is feeling like they are alone and going through these changes by themselves.

You are not alone. This awakening process has been occurring globally since the beginning of time. Here you will find an explanation of the transformations you are probably experiencing and how that ties into Spirit's ultimate plan for you. Let's start with talking about my own awakening process.

I've been intuitive since I was a child, but my most vivid memory — the starting place I refer back to for my awakening — happened on the month of my 30th birthday. I awoke one morning with a disembodied voice speaking in my ear. *"The time for playing is over. It's time to do the work you came here to do."*

Since that moment, my life has changed dramatically. Everything — love, career, and most importantly my belief system — have transformed. I have become a co-creator in my life and started to manifest the life I want.

You can manifest the life you want to. Anyone who wants to make a difference in their life can. If you ever felt like the proverbial salmon swimming against the current of life, then this book is for you. If you ever wanted to co-create your life and make your destiny; then this book is for you. And lastly, but most importantly, if you ever felt like you were destined for something more, then this book is *definitely* for you.

Take a walk with me through the steps I took in my awakening. Learn from the lessons I encountered along the way. This is the 'manual for living' we all wish we had ten-twenty years ago when we were making our foolish mistakes. Those mistakes were needed for our spiritual maturity. But what now? Here is a field guide to help you navigate this journey. This is a guide, though, and by *no* means should any of my advice supersede what you feel is accurate for you.

Each chapter includes a topic accompanied by my views on what that subject means for an awakened person. At the end of each chapter is a "Review and Journal" section for you to reflect on the reading. I am a big fan of writing, so also use this as a workbook. Take your time as you read to internalize the teachings and put your reflections into action.

Do I know everything and have all the answers for you? Certainly not. Each person's journey is different. What worked for me, may not work for you. Even if it does work, it will not be in the same combination I used. Your path may involve a little bit of insight from me, some from someone else, and then some you learned on your own. Here you become the spider, weaving your awakened home to make it comfortable for you and only you.

What I *do* know, I now offer you. Let me share the peace, contentment, happiness, joy, love, passion, fun, adventure, hope, faith and trust that now reside in my life. The fruits of the spirit come from learning who you are as an awakened being that trusts the process. These fruits are free and meant for all to enjoy.

CHAPTER 1
DESTINY AND FREE WILL

Who am I? What am I meant to be in this life? The biggest setback we encounter during awakening is dealing with our own self-imposed idea of who we are and what we can become in this lifetime.

As a self-described reading fanatic, I'm always attracted to philosophers who rebelled against popular beliefs and customs. My favorite all time novel is *Candide* by Voltaire (pen name of François-Marie Arouet) in 1759. Voltaire was a philosopher during the *Age of Enlightenment*. He was notorious for his support of freedom of religion and expression, and he was infamous for rebelling against the Catholic Church.

In his book *Candide*, Voltaire riddles another popular philosopher Leibniz who shared the theory of optimism: all works out for the best because God is a benevolent deity.

While this is a nice theory to hold on to — I even wear rose-colored glasses occasionally — the idea should *not* be forced on anyone else. At that time in society, the common man looked to philosophers for answers to life's problems. Leibniz's philosophy suggested people suffer in silence and be content with whatever his or her lot was in life.

Another of my favorite philosophers is Socrates. Known for his advanced wisdom, Socrates taught that everyone should think for himself or herself. If his teachings went against people's own judgment, he counseled that they must believe what they know, not what they were told.

Voltaire and Socrates believed in choice. They believed we have a say in how our life turns out. They taught about the power of the spirit to accomplish or manifest whatever it is we set out to have. I believe this also. It is our birthright to live the life *we want*. It is our right to have the things we desire. This is the basic Law of Attraction, the *Secret* and the idea behind the *Good Life* — we attract to ourselves what we are.

If there is free will, how does that fit in with the idea of destiny? Destiny is real, isn't it?

The online dictionary states that destiny is events that are pre-determined to happen to a particular person or certain things set to occur in the future.

I do believe in the literal definition of destiny. I think that before we come to Earth, we design this life that we are about to have. We decided the lessons we wanted to learn and the major experiences we wanted to have. I believe these things predetermine the growth of our spirit in this lifetime and help us achieve enlightenment while we're attending the earthly school.

When I say that destiny is predetermined before we get here, how then do I also support the idea of free will?

Imagine you're looking at a mapped-out traveling route. As you're looking at the overall route to reach your destination, you see definite steps in the directions that you have to make along the way. There are certain interstates, bridges, and tunnels you will use to get to your destination. As you travel, say you stop for a bathroom break, detour for a restaurant you really want to try, or veer toward a location you want to experience. Maybe you find you're tired and go off-route to a hotel in order to rest, but you travel further away to reach a certain hotel where you earn rewards.

When you turn off course for the side trips, your navigation reroutes to get you back on course to the locations you have to take in order to achieve your final destination. It may make you go further out of your way, backtrack to where you had been before, or take a much longer way to get back to where you were before you went off course. However, eventually, you will return to the same definite directions you have to make in order to reach your final designation.

In this analogy, the definite and necessary steps in the directions are destiny. The rest of the trip is free will.

Before awakening, we tend to take the long route when we travel in life. We take this longer route because we didn't know better. We weren't familiar with any shortcuts. We were inexperienced at driving. We wanted to see the scenic route. Sometimes we thought we knew better than the navigation given and ended up lost. Because of these decisions, we stretched out reaching the designated points in our destiny longer that needed.

As we awaken, becoming more conscious of life, we start to take shorter trips. We become more experienced travelers who realize how to reach our decided points in the journey faster. Because we aren't as distracted and driven off course, we end up without as much wear and tear to our traveling vehicle. We learn how to maneuver the roads easily without as much damage along the way. Even when we do bang up the vehicle of our bodies and minds during the voyage, we learn expert skills to repair the damage and get back on the road quickly.

A great example of free will and destiny unfolded during my career as a massage therapist. My destiny is to be a healer. When I was in my 30th year of life, waking to that dis-embodied message one morning, I realized I had to take action. I asked spirit to give me a sign. Later that day, I got the sudden urge to go through all of the paperwork in my desk drawer and shred old documents. I came across a scholarship I had from my days volunteering with AmeriCorps.

We weren't paid for the year of service. Instead we were given a small stipend for living expenses, and we were rewarded with a large scholarship to use for educational purposes at any accredited institution. The funny thing was, I volunteered with AmeriCorps in 2001. That meant I had exactly seven years to use the scholarship before it expired. When I rediscovered that opportunity, it was the last year I could use it. The universe was at play.

When events line up synchronously, it is a sign that something is meant to happen. This is a "turn left in 1000 feet" message from the navigation system of your destiny. I asked the universe, "Show me what you want me to do."

Within that week, I received a postcard mailer about a local massage school. Then I saw an ad about that same school on T.V. I decided to call the school to schedule a noncommittal tour that Wednesday.

Keep in mind, I was not considering going back to school for anything. I was a young stay-at-home wife with two small children under the age of five. Where would I find the time or money to continue my education? I already had a Master's Degree in Health Care Management, Bachelor's Degree in Food and Nutritional Sciences and Minor in Business Management. Why would I need more education? Logical questions always pop up when the universe is at play. When you get the "exit now" message from spirit, it is time to throw logic to the wind.

Two things happened when I went in for the tour that made me sign on the dotted line. The first was realizing that the scholarship money covered 95% of the expenses. Second, the semester started that Friday. The timing worked perfectly around my husband's and kids' schedule. In synchronicity, it was the day of my 30th birthday. I exited where destiny dictated and was returning to school.

Fast forward to when I graduated from massage school and started working my first job at a popular spa franchise. The pay was minimal and the work was hard because the demand for my work kept my schedule constantly booked. While I loved doing what I was doing, I needed to make ends meet without breaking my back. At the end of my shift, I was so tired when I arrived home that I had no energy for my kids. I decided to apply for a job at a private spa; I was hired. I was ecstatic to receive more pay for fewer hours of work. I thought that I could finally and comfortably do what I loved!

I didn't last more than three months at the private spa because the commute was horrible. I hardly had any clients. I spent most of my time sitting around, doing nothing. I was confused, trying to understand why was this was happening? I thought I followed destiny's call; why didn't it work out? It didn't work out because I executed a freewill choice.

After I resigned, I meditated to investigate why the free will choice at the new job didn't work out. I discovered that I made this decision on my own. I did not contact my guides and ask them about it, I did not tap into my higher knowing or even meditate on it! I jumped to take a detour off course because it seemed easier. I manifested the options of that second job.

I was the one who wanted to leave my spa franchise job. The new job at the private spa didn't work out because I was not meant to work for someone else. My destiny was to work for myself, doing what I love. My free will led me to take a job that — on a very small scale — because it mirrored the benefits I would achieve by following my destiny.

Learning from this lesson, whenever I make a decision now, business or personal, I meditate on it to contact my higher self in order to decide if this is what I want or need to do for my Higher Good. Every morning I always pray, "May I make decisions that are in alignment with the Highest Good of the universe, myself, and people everywhere."

On your path, you need to determine for each decision what a free will choice is and what is destiny. It isn't simple. Sometimes choices appear simple, like that second job, but you always need to keep your higher purpose in mind. Decide if that choice pulls you closer to your destiny or further away.

Destiny and free will are not cut-and-dry. All of the wrong things that happen are not because of free will choices. On the flip side, all of the good things that happen are not destiny. That is a very logical but inaccurate way of processing these two things.

When you start to delve into the mystical realm of your higher self, you have to leave your logical mind and processes behind. What we often perceive as bad can actually end up helping us, while those things that we feel are good can be damaging. The only accurate way to figure it out whether something is good or bad is time. The best thing to do when you understand that the decision is bad is to learn from that lesson and carry the knowledge with you as you journey on.

REFLECT AND JOURNAL

1) Think of three defining moments that have occurred in your life up to this point. Identify which of those choices are free will decisions and which were destiny?

_____

_____

_____

_____

_____

2) Think of a major life decision you are in the process of making right now. Contact your guides, higher self, God, and whatever spiritual guidance you depend on in prayer or meditation. Ask them if this is the right decision for you at this time. Journal the response.

_____

_____

_____

_____

_____

CHAPTER 2
DUALITY

My first steps on the spiritual path were made in baby steps. I tentatively made a comment here, posted something on Facebook there, and mentioned spiritual tidbits in passing to friends and strangers. It felt like cursing for the first time.

Do you remember those days as a teenager? When you wanted to curse but you knew it was taboo? You spit out your first curse to just say it out loud regardless of appropriateness, conversation, timing, or sound. You started tentatively testing the new word out around new people to gage their reactions. When they approved, your confidence to try to use that word more often or try another grew. If they looked alarmed, you drew back, knowing that wasn't a safe place to continue expanding your vocabulary.

During the newly awakened stage of my life, I learned the meaning of *Namaste* and knew it was the greeting I wanted to use with people. *Namaste* translates to mean, "The Divine Spark which is within me honors the Divine Spark that is within you too." Using this phrase felt right because I was beginning to see past the personalities of people to recognize the light within them. My understanding was grasping that we're all souls that come from the same place for a human experience. The greeting felt like a natural extension of that acknowledgement.

When I first spoke the greeting out loud to another person, I was terrified. My mental chatter was in overdrive, "What will people think? What if they ask me the meaning and I forget? What if they look at me funny? Am I supposed to put my hands in prayer format? Would that look strange?"

As with cursing, I persisted. I chose my audience carefully. If the person was Indian, it came more naturally for me to say, "Namaste." People from India understand the meaning of the greeting and the intent behind it. With everyone else, I faltered because my insecurities were at play. What I found was that the transition started to happen simply because there was a desire within me for it to occur. I just had to sort out my ego from the spiritual practice.

Metaphysical circles talk about the two parts of a person in terms of ego and spirit. The spirit part of a person is the soul and it comes from the light and love above. The ego is the human part of a person and includes the personality, emotions, and feelings.

As your journey down a spiritual path progresses, the spirit side starts to take over and ego starts to takes a back seat. The full transition to check ego at the door and walk each day in spirit takes a while. The time it takes depends on how attached a person is to their ego self. If you really are embarking on a spiritual path to further your evolvement, then you have the right intention, and the space will be provided for you to naturally outgrow your ego.

One of the ways I can tell if ego is involved with my clientele is if I hear any of these three things:

- I NEED to know my life path and life purpose now!
- I HAVE to start my spiritual business now!
- A reader/psychic/shaman told me I will be a great reader/psychic/ shaman etc...
- I was told I am meant to be on the spiritual path

Do you see the common theme? There is always a sense of urgency and importance. The spiritual self is not concerned with these things. It is concerned with peace, happiness and joy; all things that can be developed within someone at their own pace and for their own pleasure. Yet somehow, that knowledge is not enough.

I have been the owner of a spiritual wellness center for over ten years and every year I meet someone with these same thoughts and remarks. One lady in particular got to me because every class she attended, she kept going on and on about how spirit required her to start her spiritual business but she didn't know where to start or how to begin. In one class after we spent enough time dissecting her root issue, I stated the question to the class to ponder:

"If spirit was in such a rush to get you working in the spiritual field, wouldn't you be doing so already?"

Also let's take ego out of it. There are plenty of amazing healers and practitioners around right NOW, why not send the people you know needing help to them? If you know of an awesome healer, why would you keep them from your friend who needs help now?

If you are strutting down the spiritual path in search of recognition or to stand out, you're feeding the ego over the spirit and you may stumble more along the way.

What transpires is a transition process. A testing process ensues to determine what works for you and what doesn't. The start of my spiritual voyage came with the realization that going to church every Sunday was not necessary. While experimenting with sharing my new taboo phrases and experiences, I also learned I had to start weeding out some people from my inner circle. I realized I needed to find new, spiritually uplifting friends who were also dedicated to awakening.

Where this was the start of my spiritual evolution, your conversion may be different. An awakened path is an intuitive path. Our individual souls choose and select the experiences that are needed to foster growth, experience, and ascension.

One important thing to remember is that your process is uniquely your own. You can't explain it to anyone. A friend helped me realize this when we were discussing my new life changes. She said, "I just let you talk and figure it out because I really don't know what to say to you. And even if I did say something, you will still do what you feel is right to do for you"

I loved her for that. I was trying so hard to make sense of all the changes taking place. When I tried to convey that to someone else, my explanations came across as wishy-washy or scattered. Luckily, that friend knew me all my life. She knew I wasn't all over the place or indecisive.

The early part of an awakening is a good time to understand the vulnerability that can come with how other people perceive your transformation. I would love to say to you, "People's reactions don't matter." I tell my clients and students, "Don't let someone else's opinions define your reality."

But I know better. I know that experiencing the major life changes that come with awakening create a scary time. The last thing you need as your entire belief system and reality is shifting are unsupportive comments or derogatory smirks. My personal and professional advice to avoid is — don't share your journey with anyone else unless you have proven trust in them. Get in the habit of writing in a journal and sharing your journey there. Writing is an awesome process, especially in retrospect when you look back through your journal to see just how far you have really come.

At the beginning of my spiritual revolution, I based my path on the Yogic discipline. Once I became more comfortable with my practice, I started posting on Facebook about my meditation sessions and yoga classes. However, being the free spirit that I am, I was also posting girls' night out pictures and parties. This is one part of the transition people don't want to talk about.

While you are moving into your own space and becoming who you are destined to be, there are still remnants from your past that remain part of you. As a reformed party girl from the Caribbean, it is in my blood to move to the music and groove on a night out with my closest friends.

Soon after posting about my new spiritual practices and some of these random nights out with my friends, an old friend messaged me. He wanted to know what religion I was practicing. I told him, "I'm spiritual. I'm not practicing any religion."

His response was, "You're not spiritual. How can you call yourself spiritual and still drink, party with friends, have casual relationships, and enjoy a good time?"

Fear rose up inside of me. Maybe he was right. How could I do all of these things at the same time? I must be awful for saying I'm spiritual while I still live life to the fullest. It didn't matter that my time out was harmless fun with decadent behavior. I readied to reply with an apology for the error of my foolish ways. Then a very calm and grounded voice inside asked, "What does being spiritual have to do with having fun?"

"It has everything to do with it! You can't do it," I answered.

"Why not?" the voice questioned.

"I don't know," I pondered. "It's just immoral."

Spirit pointed out something crucial to understand. My friend was not mad at me for partying. He was living on Fear Street. This fear about his own life led him to make judgments about my life.

Of course people can have fun. Evolving spiritually should add more joy to your life not take it away. Being spiritual is about having a close personal relationship with God — and depending on your beliefs — that God can be outside of you or within you.

The dualism of awakening is very similar to how people get into a serious relationship and feel like they have to stop living outside of that connection. I was never one to do so, but many people believe that in a steady relationship any life outside of that relationship should cease to exist.

Loving God and loving life are not separate. These things go hand-in-hand. The more we laugh and experience joy, the more it pleases God because we're relishing in His creation and the experiences of it.

Even though I've changed a lot of my eating, drinking, and social habits since the start of my awakening, this has nothing to do with me becoming more spiritual. The change in food, drink, and habits has to do with the demands of my work as a psychic medium and healer.

There is no right or wrong way to be spiritual as there is no right or wrong way to lay healing hands. I've met and interacted with some of the most amazing healers. My circle of gifted healers runs the gamut from the sincerely austere that are practicing vegans, celibate, and profound meditators, to those who drink wine, smoke weed, and *Party Like It's 1999* crazy people. Each one provides good services to their clients and loved ones when it comes time to heal.

Following your path authentically means that your growth will be more intuitive and less organized. If spirit determines you need to be vegetarian to do a certain kind of work, then you will denounce all meat. If spirit decides you need more iron in your diet, you will crave a steak like it's no one's business.

I don't know what spirit will require of me later on in my practice. It's quite possible that thirty years from now I will have another completely different diet and social agenda. But for now, I do find that a lot of rest and a mostly vegetarian diet support what is needed for my healing and psychic abilities. The child in me loves whenever my friends and I get away for a weekend. I still indulge in the occasional steak and dance-a-thon till midnight.

You have to recognize the duality of being alive. Your spirit self requires certain behaviors to make it happy. Your ego self requires almost the opposite to be content. The choice is up to you — and only you — how you find balance in your life.

The transition process from your 'old' self to the 'new' self is particularly hard for everyone because people don't understand duality. Some people in your life still remember you as you always were before; they can be a little cynical about the change to who you are now. When you need comfort, just remember that even Jesus was chased out of his hometown!

People who have known you all your life may have a hard time accepting that you are growing in a new direction. Try to remember that their fear of the unknown is a very big fear. Their disposition towards you has nothing to do with you; it is a reflection of their own insecurities. Deep down it may be their own wish to make changes in their own lives and their courage hasn't yet met their desire. It's imperative during your infancy of awakening to have a lot of compassion and understanding when interacting with these people. Witnessing your transformation could be just the thing they need to begin transforming their lives as well.

Awakening in life does not necessarily mean making a specific choice in lifestyles and behaviors. You must be authentic to what feels right. Otherwise, you're not walking your spiritual path, but traveling another's.

While we're all on a path heading in the same direction, each person's path is unique. Some people may be ahead of you or behind you. Some may walk their road vastly different from any way you could imagine. No judgment should come from you; no judgment should be accepted by you. Be content in the here-and-now, as well as the duality, of where you are. Know that soon enough, more changes will come as you continue developing into who you were meant to be.

REFLECT AND JOURNAL

1) Do you struggle with the duality of being spiritual and still having fun? Give an example.

_____

_____

_____

_____

_____

2) Has anyone criticized you for this kind of duality? How would you handle the situation differently after reading this?

_____

_____

_____

_____

_____

CHAPTER 3
THE LONE WOLF

When we awaken to our life's purpose, we automatically make a decision to stop following the path everyone else is on. We start to evaluate what works for us and what doesn't.

When people ask me where I am from, I like to cheekily say, "The World." It's partly true! I was born in London, England and grew up in the Caribbean and South American before moving to the United Stated. In terms of religion, I feel too I have been them all.

My father's family is Hindu so I was born Hindu. My mother was Muslim and between these two crazy kids, they decided to send me to church every Sunday with my Anglican Aunt Iris. I remember my childhood filled with Easter weekend church services, Lenten periods of fast, pujas at family homes and Ramadan fasting and going to mosque with my mom. It was a well-balanced childhood because in dabbling with all these religions, I learned at a young and early age that no one was wrong, every path was right and I loved them all.

At the time of my awakening, I was Non-Denominational Christian attending a Baptist church locally in my town. When I got off the Christian path, I stepped away from the *religious* path. I realized I was on my own.

There are millions of people who live in a spiritual instead of a religious way. At the start of my transformation, I didn't know a single one. Everyone in my social group was part of the church I went to. When I decided to start a different path, I had no idea how to navigate that transition with my friends.

I remember the first Sunday I decided not to go to church. I lay in bed, waiting for the fire and brimstone to fall from the sky. God was surely going to let me have it for being disobedient. Nothing happened.

Life continued on without the wrath of God. For our household, it was a little bit brighter because there was no mad Sunday dash to church with crying children, an unkempt house, and me wearing uncomfortable heels to fit in with the rest of the church-going women.

That first Sunday at home was spent making pancakes for my kids while listening to Bob Marley — a tribute to my Caribbean heritage. I felt peaceful and content like God met me where I resided.

Please know that I am not knocking religion or criticizing conformity. If you attend church and you look forward to the Sunday service every weekend, then you are being authentic to what you love. God resides there for you. Continue that practice because that is where He will find you and commune with you.

For me, He found me right in the comfort of my home while I was washing dishes and listening to *No Woman No Cry*. I knew without question that I made the right choice.

Being an awakened being is a lot like becoming poster child for the unconventional. We must also dally in some black magic arts because we are no longer tied to the fear that makes people do things they don't care to do. My newfound courage to blaze down a new path was shunned and my church friends started dropping away one by one.

At that time, I was part of a mom's group from my church. We had a Mother of Preschoolers (MOPs) program at the church that met once a month for fellowship and breakfast. I was second in charge to assist the MOPs leader at these events. When the program started, we had over thirty women signed up with their children. We had to divide the women into five groups. At every meeting we had five tables set up to accommodate the groups. Once assigned to a group, a person would remain in that group for a semester (like school, MOPs ran from September-May).

At our first meeting, I bonded immediately with the women at my table. They were vivacious, fun, and loved to laugh. We were all mothers to little boys — not one of us had a girl child! We became the MOB group (Mothers of Boys). When MOPS ended for summer, we continued to meet once a month for GNO (Girls Night Out). We also hosted play dates and get-togethers at our homes so we, and our children, could interact while MOPs was on hiatus.

It was at the end of one MOPs season, before the start of the other, when my husband and I separated. I broke the news to my group of friends over lunch. Everyone was shocked; stunned in contemplative silence.

One woman spoke up and let me know that she would pray for me. She suggested for my husband and not to worry, all will be well, and we will work it out. That left me shocked. She didn't even ask if I was all right or if this was a decision I made. She assumed he made the request as if I was at his disposal. I gently let her know that I was the one who requested a divorce; it was my decision to separate. The silence deepened.

We eventually changed the topic. Some of the women remained noticeably uncomfortable around me. In turn, I felt the same toward them.

Soon after that lunch, one of the women reached out to me, asking if she could come by for a play date. I happily agreed. I knew no one else in Virginia. If I lost my church friends, I would really be alone.

After we settled the kids to their activities, we decided to play a game of Scrabble. We were having a good time, catching up and chatting, when very nonchalant she asked, "What's your relationship with Jesus Christ at this point?"

Initially I didn't respond because I was dumbfounded. The thought hadn't crossed my mind that Jesus and I broke up because I left the Church. As some say, I was feeling some kinds of way about this intrusion. I was hurt that she questioned my sincere love for Jesus. I was angry that she was prying into my personal business. I was also confused — what if she was right? What if Jesus was mad at me because I left his Father's establishment?

The confusing emotions dissipated, being replaced by serenity. A sense of peace washed over me. I sat up straighter, looking her straight in her eyes to say, "My relationship with Jesus is just fine. We decided to stop playing pretend in front of everyone at church and now have an open and honest relationship at home."

This charming little spirit-sent quip didn't end the conversation there. Instead, it fueled my friend into an interrogation that would have put the Spanish Inquisition to shame. Armed with her in-depth knowledge of the Bible, she presented a well thought out case to demonstrate the error of my ways. It ended with the showstopper of how negatively this decision would affect my children.

Serenity became panic. Calm turned to anxiety. An annoying little voice — not the one I had been faithfully following for the past several months — started screeching, "What if she's right? What if she's right?"

To quell that voice, another calm, centered, and powerful voice came forward. In that instant the distinction was made between friend and foe. Armed with its backup, I spoke my truth.

"I can understand your deep love and devotion for the Christian path. You were brought up in it and your whole family and all your friends are in it. It is a simple choice for you and in fact, not really a choice at all. The decision was made once you were born, and there you have stayed faithfully. However, staying on a path you were automatically put on, does not speak anything to your devotion. If you want to show me devotion, then leave the church. Dabble in other faiths, learn their ways and customs and then come back into your faith. If you are fully resolved this is the path for you, then I commend you on being a devoted Christian."

Unlike the theme of congruent oneness with one religion in her life, I was born Hindu to an atheist father and Muslim mother. I grew up Anglican and was therefore baptized and confirmed.

Through the years, I followed the Buddhist, Baha'i, Pagan, Wiccan and Non-Denominational Christian paths before stepping on the Yogic Path. Since then, I've been devoted to the Yogic Path because it is the right choice for me. This path does not condemn anyone and that's important to me.

Being Christian in a family of Atheists, Hindus, Muslims and Baha'is brought a sense of sadness. If I was the only one going to heaven, what was the point? Why couldn't my family go, too? They are all good people.

Though my dad doesn't do pujas or go to church, he is one of the most charitable people I know. He is always giving money to help a cause, foundation, or school team. The idea that God would deny anyone entrance into heaven because other faiths didn't get the memo about Jesus didn't sit well with me. Who made up these rules anyways?!

We muddled through the rest of that Scrabble game. When she left with kids in tow, we both knew it was the end of our friendship. It was bittersweet, because while I was relieved not to have to defend my right to live the way I wanted to, I was sad to lose a friend over my choice. This pattern repeated throughout the next couple of years not only with friends, but also with family members.

Claiming the awakened path is a lonely road in the beginning. Please don't think you have to sell your home and occupy some space on a mountain to live the awakened life. You just have to be strong enough to stand strong in your conviction that you are doing the best thing for yourself. When you are firmly planted in *your* truth, the universe will reward you.

When awakening, you are tuning in to what *you* need to evolve in your life. You start to merge into being part of that coveted ideal of being "one with the universe." Your awareness becomes conscious of what it takes for your organism to survive.

Part of that survival includes cutting people off and moving on to a better crowd. This is different from cutting negative people out of your life. Sometimes the crowd you are moving away from is not negative at all. You just have such different viewpoints on life it's hard to find common ground.

I'm not saying you can't be friends with people of different viewpoints, but if you are, they *must* be respectful of your beliefs and support you. It does no good to continually surround yourself with people who are highly opinionated and feel their way is the best way. Every person needs a support system that allows them to live life their way.

The theme of duality will come up and my advice is to make friends with it, do not feel guilty and be bold in sharing your duality with others. It's ok to go back and forth in your choices as you pick out the path and the life best suited for you. If anything, be like Samantha from the popular TV show called *Sex in the City*. The time had come for her to break up with her boyfriend and her famous last words to him were, "*I do love you Jared but I love me more.*"

Be a Samantha. Chose you, love you and honor you, duality and all.

REFLECT AND JOURNAL

1) Can you see the duality theme in your life now? Describe how it shows up in your life:

_____

_____

_____

_____

_____

2) Describe a time in your life when you had to let go of a relationship that no longer served you. How did it make you feel?

_____

_____

_____

_____

_____

CHAPTER 4
SANGHA

In Matthew 12:43-45 in the New Testament of the Bible it says, "When an impure spirit comes out of a person, it goes through arid places seeking rest and does not find it. Then it says, 'I will return to the house I left.' When it arrives, it finds the house unoccupied, swept clean and put in order. Then it goes and takes with it seven other spirits more wicked than itself, and they go in and live there. And the final condition of that person is worse than the first."

When teaching, I apply this proverb to habits. Let's say you have the habit of smoking and you want to quit. To quit, you go cold turkey, cutting cigarettes from your life. Based on shear willpower, you manage to stay clean for two weeks. Now think of that addiction in the form of an impure spirit that left your body. If you do not replace your old addiction with new and healthy behaviors, it will return. When it comes back, it will bring friends in the form of other addictions like overeating or pornography.

Through the example may be extreme, you get the basic idea. When we cut something out of our life, we have to replace it in order to fill the hole created by the absence. If we do not, then we leave space open for something to come in that may be worse than the initially initial habit.

Through the process of awakening, when you realize that some of your friends or family are not healthy for you, you start limiting your interactions with them. Then you will come to a point when you need to find new people to socialize with that will fill that need for social relationships.

I love groups like Meetup.com. They offer the opportunity for people to get together at an event or location based on mutual interests. When I first discovered Meetup, I signed up for over thirty clubs. After signing up, I became a sideline observer. I hardly went to gatherings and only participated via internet participation. I agreed with the idea of meeting new people; however, the idea of actually stepping outside of my comfort zone to connect to strangers was frightening. What would they think of me? How would I fit in? What if they don't like me?

Obsessive thoughts swirled in my mind, convincing me to stay in the comfort of my cozy home. I was proud of myself for signing up to be part of the groups; I didn't need to actually follow through with connecting to the people there.

Finally, a group close to me posted an event that perked my interest. While I was interested, fear prevented me from RSVP'ing. For that first week, I denied my interest, making up excuses to reinforce why I shouldn't go. But one thing you will learn is that spirit is persistent. When it comes to furthering your growth, spirit can be unrelenting. I was nagged and reminded about the event so often so that I finally gave in out of exasperation. I planned to go for an hour before quietly slipping out when no one was looking.

This group I attended was hosting a Reiki share experience in Springfield. When I arrived, I was immediately blown away by the accepting and gracious nature of the host. To this day, when I think of David, my heart melts. Since the first day we met, I realized he is one of the most empathetic people I have ever met. That first day, he was so warm and inviting; welcoming me into his home like we have been friends forever. I knew spirit was at work because all of my fears and insecurities vanished when David smiled at me and welcomed me to his home. I could feel that my journey was going to change from that moment forward, but it was going to be okay because spirit guided me to a place where I would be nurtured.

At that first event, I met other happy and enlightened healers. Two women, Ma Mary and Ma Frieda stood out to me. Being with them felt like being home with family. Carolyn Myss talks about people being archetypes; I knew that these two women were mother archetypes for me. I felt things from them that was reminiscent of my childhood — unconditional love and acceptance.

For the first time in a long time, I felt like I was free to be me. That freedom became one of the reasons I grew to become a successful healer today. To have people stand beside you, supporting you and believing in you, is very empowering. It truly takes your work, goals, and vision to a higher level.

These three individuals, along with Reverend Ric, became my new family. For a long time, I attended that group every month, excited to heal and be healed with this wonderful group of people. Outside of the meetings, we became friends, leaning on and supporting each other during hard times.

As I was going through my divorce, I was torn because the influence of religious beliefs made me feel like I was disappointing God. It was Reverend Ric who took my hand and delivered the most dazzling smile as I cried heavily. He asked, "Who said God is upset with you? All He wants is for you to be happy, sweetheart."

Those words still come back to replay as fresh as if I were still sitting there with Reverend Ric holding my hand. It was a profound truth — God wants me to be happy because he created me. He wants his creation to be happy. Astounding — no judgment, just acceptance.

Bonding with an amazing group of strangers that understood me at the soul level changed me. That was what I was missing with my old group of friends. I was craving that acceptance, understanding and shared knowing of what I felt. My old group of friends loved me, but they were too entwined in my life yet not far enough in to see me. Having fresh faces in life that are there to support you without judgment is powerful. Spirit knew to lead me to these people, and as a result I grew tremendously.

When I hear people say that they don't need people to grow, I know I'm hearing someone who takes the long road to enlightenment. I once knew a woman who was celibate for three years and in that time she told me she healed her emotional pain and baggage of relationships. I smiled. I told her the first relationship she gets into, will put her right back at the beginning.

Sure enough, a couple of months went by and then she asked to see me. She did get in a relationship and she felt awful! It's like she learned nothing in the past three years because she was back to being insecure, whiny and jealous!

You can't learn how to deal with people by working on yourself and being alone. That's like saying I am a pilot because I read a manual on how to fly a plane! People and relationships teach us many things. We learn through the interaction. We can learn the hard way by dealing with difficult relationships or, by my understanding, we can learn the easy way by cultivating healthy relationships based on trust, understanding, and acceptance. The best training that comes in healthy connections is always love, complete and unconditional love.

When I experienced new and profound things with this new group of friends, no one scoffed, belittled, or made fun of me. They either related to my experiences or knew who to direct me to for guidance and support. This supported my growth individually and as a healer.

Here you are growing spiritually. If it hasn't already been, it will be required to let go of old relationships that no longer serve you. That isn't meant as a sign to live in solitude as a hermit. As quickly as those old relationships are removed, new ones will be supplied to foster your growth. Just trust in this; let go of your fear or insecurities. Put yourself out there to find your community — your Sangha. I promise you, it will further your growth in more ways than one.

REFLECT AND JOURNAL

1) Take a dare! Join one group this week that is completely out of your comfort zone but shares mutual interests with you. Sign up today! Journal your experiences as you go through this process.

_____

_____

_____

_____

_____

2) As you're meeting new people, try to cultivate a more accepting attitude and be less judgmental of those you meet. How did this change your experience?

_____

_____

_____

_____

_____

CHAPTER 5
RELATIONSHIPS

Many times I see clients struggling with personal relationships. Since this is a sensitive subject, I will try to be delicate in the discussion after approaching one truth — all your relationships reflect what you are.

Relationships are lessons for soul growth. Relationships develop with people to mirror what we need to work on in ourselves. Here is a personal example — in one year I dated two compulsive liars back-to-back. The lesson from those relationships was the realization that I was not being authentic. I was living a lie by not living true to myself. Because of my own dishonesty with myself, I only attracted liars for relationships.

Relationships, as I refer to them, are not limited to strictly love relationships. Every connection we have with friends, coworkers, family, or social groups are relationships that teach us.

A former female client complained that everyone in her life was jealous of her. Her mother, her aunts, her girlfriends all made life miserable for her. In her mind, this happened because of jealousy. My advice was, "Stop being jealous and they will too."

She denied it. "I'm not a jealous person."

We went to the drawing board to evaluate her life. By the end of the exercise, she started to discover ways that she was judging people. Being a very ambitious woman, watching successful people motivated her to climb the ladder of success to achieve the same. However, she wasn't cognizant of what she really wanted in life. The lack of clear direction led to her goals being derailed and treated as petty. Her reaction to this was being jealous of others' success. The antidote to rectify the situation was to rejoice in the success of others and be happy for their accomplishments. Then that positive energy should become the motivation to help her achieve her goals.

People get upset when discussing this mirror philosophy. It is understandable because this exercise takes the negative energy they're placing on someone else and reflects it back in a way that doesn't paint them in the best light.

"What don't you like about this person?" I asked clients.

"She is too snobby and thinks she knows it all."

"Okay," I respond. "What if I was to say you are describing traits within yourself that you do not like and want to work on?"

"No, that's not me at all. That is her."

When we separate from another person, we deny our very existence. We are all part of one another. What we notice around us in our perceptions is really based on our own inner reality.

It's important to remember that we are spiritual beings having a human experience. The human experience is all about growing. This planet is the earth school where we came to learn and develop.

Taking this understanding into consideration, we gain perspective on why relationships end. Once we have learned all we need to from that person, the need to be with them diminishes. This is why I generally say nothing when my friends enter in to unhealthy relationships. I know there is a big lesson there. Depending on how awakened they are, it may take days, weeks, months, or years for that lesson to be learned. I had a friend date a man for over ten years and she still hadn't absorbed her lessons from him. To this day, she is still attached to him in some way.

For my readers in monogamous relationships, have no fear that the need for your significant other will diminish once you've learned your lesson from them. Doreen Virtue, a gifted healer and published author, teaches that we can exercise our choice to stay with our mates even after we learned our lessons.

What she taught can be seen in the majority of marriages that start off rough, but twenty years later the couple is peaceful and happy. They learned their lessons and decided to stay together, choosing to learn the remainder of their lessons from others together.

Once you've adopted this attitude that all of life is learning, then you will be less emotional and attached to the outcome of your relationships. You will understand that the only constant in the universe is change. Your spirit will develop to be adventurous and take on each new challenge willingly.

Attachments are a complicated part of relationships. I love each religious path for the different insight and knowledge they bring. What I love about the Buddhist path is the Four Noble Truths that teach about attachments when it states:

1) Life is suffering
2) The origin of suffering is attachment
3) The cessation of suffering is attainable
4) There is a path that leads to the cessation of suffering

Following this reasoning, we can begin to explore how our attachments to people and things bring about suffering. Think about it, when you are not enjoying life, it is usually at the end of a relationship, a pleasurable activity, or a certain job description.

Many times when discussing relationships with my clients, it is easy to relate this concept to relationships outside of romantic love like work or family relationships. However, once we shift to the topic of romantic love, defenses rise and people are less open to accept the idea of learning lessons and moving on. Their idea of romantic love centers around being attached to that person.

My views on attachment in relationships, otherwise known as monogamy, have changed since my awakening. Now I understand that monogamy may not be for everyone. If someone is having a hard time holding down a relationship, have no fear, there is a reason why.

Speaking for myself, I am constantly changing. I'm in a perpetual state of evolving as I learn from spirit and become more awakened. I change direction often to adjust to my soul path's needs. In the midst of these changes, my behavior will change. What I require changes too. Many times in my relationships, my partner is not willing to change with me or they cannot change. That's when fights ensue. Should I stay the same to stay with him? Should I honor my path, allowing the change to happen, knowing fully well it will pull me away from him? More often than not, I decide to continue evolving and part ways with my lover.

Monogamy has a very notorious past based on some interesting theories. Some people say it was devised by the Roman Catholic church in its early days when priests were allowed to have many wives (as was the custom of the day). When the priests died, the church was expected to take care of the large families. Because this added a significant financial burden, the church made priests take only one wife, and then none at all.

Before the church, in humankinds early days when we moved as pack animals, the survival of the pack relied on depending on each other. There was no such thing as one family unit. The pack was the family unit. When women had babies, the pack raised the child in the same spirit of the African proverb, "It takes a village to raise a child."

When I didn't know anything else, I was all for monogamy. My mom and dad are still married to this day. The culture I was raised in supported monogamy. However, my interactions with clients are continually inspiring more awakening. Once I met a couple that changed my whole idea of relationships.

This couple was a married couple that was also polyamorous. While the idea sounded very cool and modern, I couldn't wrap my head wrap around some concepts. How do you handle jealousy? What does one spouse do if the other spouse goes on a date with another person?

The husband explained, "We are all realizing that we come from the same place. We are one with Spirit. There is no difference and in fact, religion teaches us to treat everyone equally. How can we live that idea if we choose one person over another to be with in a monogamous relationship?"

In their example, issues of jealousy and insecurity were personal issues that need to be worked through personally. If two people fully support the idea that they love each other equally, it's a very awakened idea that they should not have preferences nor be expected to be placed on a pedestal over all other. Though that view may not be right for everyone, it is congruent with the idea of oneness where we avoid segregating ourselves as different from ourselves.

Later in my dating life, I found more examples of polyamory. I met some astounding men who were gorgeous, successful, full of love and affection, on top of being polyamorous. They did not see the need to settle down. These men were fascinating because they were living the dream. They were highly intelligent and successful. The one thing they all had in common was the choice to date with no rush to settle down with one woman.

Your ideal for relationships should be a unique and private decision made by you for you. It shouldn't be determined by your family, your religion, and definitely not by society. Today you may be polyamorous; tomorrow you may be monogamous. Whatever, decision you make, just remember two things:

1) All relationships are meant to help you develop in wisdom and insight. Use the experiences wisely. If it should end, practice non-attachment to let go.
2) Remain authentic in your decision-making. Whatever decisions you make about relationships, make those choices for yourself with no regret or apology to anyone else.

REFLECT AND JOURNAL

1) Make a list of three difficult relationships in your life. Describe what you don't like about the each person. How does that pertain to you?

_____

_____

_____

_____

_____

2) Are there any relationships from your past that provided important learning experiences and now the connection is no longer in your life?

_____

_____

_____

_____

_____

CHAPTER 6
BATTLING FEAR

If you didn't mysteriously jump to this chapter in order to read it before all of the others (maybe guided by spirit), then you will see an underlying theme that's been discussed so far — fear. People are fearful and fear is everywhere; this world at this time is a frightful place.

In the early days of my awakening, I hosted a group of wonderful women who met at my house every Thursday night. We were all starting out on our paths and met to practice using our gifts and learn new things to help us grow. I called us the Lotus Petals because, if you know me, you know I am obsessed with all things lotus flower.

Each week, we would break bread and chat about how we incorporated new things from our awakenings into our week. We would do Reiki healing on each other, listen to guided meditations, or try to read each other for practice.

One night, we started having some intense spiritual experiences. The temperature dropped to freezing around us. We were spooked! Suddenly, there was a knock on the door. I screamed, jumping behind my friend Carol. She refused to go see who was at the door alone. We huddled together and shuffled to the door. When we saw a lady outside, we both screamed again. Was she a ghost? Are we both seeing her? Eventually, we built up the courage to open the door. Carol squeaked out, "Can we help you?"

The lady looked us up and down, answering, "Yeah, I live up the street and just wanted you to know that your garage door is open. You might want to close that." She appraised us again like we were weirdoes. Then I realized why. I was almost riding Carol piggyback as she held her mouth closed in fear. I climbed off Carol and thanked my neighbor for her concern. I hoped she didn't share that experience with the rest of the neighborhood – talk about being the crazy neighbor.

As you awaken, your intuitive and psychic senses automatically start to open. You give the universe permission to be used as a vessel. That being said, if your vessel is well equipped to interact with spirits, sense things, or see visions, then you may want to brace yourself for the whole new plethora of information coming your way.

In Gary Zukav's book *Spiritual Partnerships*, he talks about human beings evolving from five sensory individuals to multisensory individuals. We use our five senses — sight, sound, smell, touch, taste — in combination with intuition and gut instinct to gain a more profound understanding of what's around us.

As we evolve in our awakening, we begin to recognize and use our gifts for the higher good of the universe, including ourselves. What you need to know about being a vessel for spirit communication is this; you no longer have control over who contacts you or why they do. You may have control over the session you give but even then, sometimes negative energy can affect us no matter how much you protect yourself.

One night I was cooking in the kitchen, making mashed potatoes. My boys were running around the island playing catch. I looked down to see Joshua run away laughing from someone that was hiding by my leg. It was a little boy wearing a red long sleeve shirt. He was in spirit. While it unnerved me, it had no effect on Joshua who just thought of him as his little friend playing catch. That night out of fear, I left all the lights on in the house when I went to bed.

When your intuitive senses open, you may begin to see things out of the corner of your eye or hear your name whispered close to your ear. You will have sudden bursts of insight or know things you never knew before. When these things happen, try not to doubt it or tell yourself you are making it up. I am here to tell you, as a well-established psychic healer, we all battle with that fear of your supernatural communications being imagination every day. You can believe that fearful voice. Or you can do as I do, simply acknowledge the fear, separate from it, and continue your psychic work.

Once I attended a weekend seminar at Edgar Cayce's A.R.E. in Virginia Beach, Virginia with three amazing psychics and healers, Echo Bodine, Judith

Pennington and Lynn Robinson. Their gifts were astounding. But Lynn really found a special space in my heart. Sharing her talents, she travelled all around the world, rubbing elbows with celebrities like Deepak Chopra and Anderson Cooper. At this weekend seminar, she completely admitted that she still battled with fear and disbelief over her experiences. She also questioned if she made up the information she received and experienced or if it really happened. If someone as talented and recognized as Lynn Robinson still questions this gift, who are we to do otherwise?

Until we live in a world where intuitive people are valued and respected for their craft, we will always question being fake or artificial. If it is going to take a while for the world to come around to what we already know, that spirits do exist and we have a connection to the other side, then we might as well get comfy and learn to let go of the fear and invite love into our hearts.

I tell my students that there are two basic emotions: love and fear. You cannot live on Fear Street and Love Avenue. Sometimes some say they can have a house on the intersection. Really think about that — your address is only going to be one of those streets. So which is it for you?

When you live in love, there is nothing scary about the earth experience anymore. Everything is wonderful and you pretty much wear rose-colored glasses plastered to your head.

When people insult you, you think back to their childhood and how it must have been rough growing up with condescending parents. When your boyfriend lies to you about having a terminal illness, you feel sorry that he felt he needed to make up such a big lie to get attention. When your friend makes it her business to go around telling everyone you are a fake and an imposter just because you had to let her unhealthy friendship go, you wish her well and pray for her to grow and mature spiritually regardless of her actions.

I live on Love Avenue. I can honestly say I hold no grudge towards anyone who has purposefully caused me harm. Like Jesus said, "Forgive them Father for they know not what they do." People living unconsciously cannot be held accountable for their actions.

The problem is while I live on Love Avenue and live consciously, I am not the poster child for living on Love Avenue. This is another misconception we have to banish. Living in love does not and should not bring up images of happy, hippy, peace-loving people picking flowers. I am blunt, straightforward, and honest to a fault. The way I show love is through honesty. I will not lie to you; in fact, more often than not, I hurt people's feelings because I tell the truth plainly. I do this out of love.

A lot of spiritually unconscious people who bring hurt and pain into your life have no idea of how their actions affect you. So bless them. Forgive them and keep it moving. One day, in the beauty of life, they will reflect on the situation and remember and feel remorse. They will desire your forgiveness and will receive it in the form of acceptance and clarity. That is, *if* you already bestowed it upon them. At that moment, no matter where you are in the world, you will have a sudden feeling of love and acceptance envelop you. It all works out for everyone in the end, so why wait? Start living on Love Avenue today. It will only enhance your life for the better.

REFLECT AND JOURNAL

1) Where do you live? Fear Street or Love Avenue?

_____

_____

_____

_____

_____

_____

_____

_____

_____

2) Describe a time your psychic gifts opened up suddenly. What did you experience? How did you feel?

_____

_____

_____

_____

_____

_____

_____

_____

_____

Do you struggle with fear? If so, do you feel better knowing that we all experience the same thing?

_____

_____

_____

_____

_____

_____

_____

_____

_____

_____

CHAPTER 7
Ego Rising

Even awakened people can go astray, get bamboozled, and run amuck. Some walk around like they are God's gift to everyone, strutting like a proud peacock, because they're awakened and have learned to be a multisensory person.

By *some* people — I of course — mean me.

It's a head-trip when you lay hands and see miracles happen. When you have someone sob with relief over receiving comfort they have sought for years, it's elating. When you see the light bulb of insight go off in a person's mind, realizing the power of something you said, it's a rush. The disappearance of pain, anguish, emotional or mental upheaval due to your work can create a heady affect. On top of all that, they turn to you saying those dreaded words, "Thank you for healing and helping me."

We're not all called to be Mother Theresa here. Even she was extremely humble until her last day on earth. The majority of us are regular people who awakened spontaneously. We were watching MTV cribs and wishing for that big mansion next to Jay Z and Beyoncé too and wondering what exactly is a vacation on the French Riviera like. We bought into the "American Dream," just like everyone else. We didn't think it was within arm's reach.

When we become awakened, people notice and eventually begin turning to us for healing, insight, wisdom, and help. It can be a real ego-trip.

I remember clearly a healing session I had at a local spa franchise. The woman booked a massage and told me to stay clear from her lower back. I obliged, but as I was working around the rest of her back, she began to tell me the story about her low back.

"It's the strangest thing, if anyone comes anywhere near this spot on my left side, I jump!" I didn't think anything of it as more than residual pain until she mentioned an interesting fact.

"When I was a child I had a spinal tap done and it was a very traumatic experience. However, I clearly remember them doing it on the right side, but my family always told me I must have forgotten because the pain is clearly on the left."

Warning bells started going off immediately. She didn't forget. The memory of that traumatic incident was stored in her back on that spot on the left. It was not a physical wound; it was a psychic wound.

I asked her if she ever had it evaluated. She explained that she had visited numerous healers to no avail. I asked her if I could do some healing work on the area. I mentioned Reiki and briefly described how it worked. She was open to and agreed to include it in our session.

Closing my eyes, I cleared my head. I initiated the Reiki flow, hovering over the spot because I didn't want to get too close and send her cringing off the table. As I felt the Reiki moving through the spot, I instinctively felt her energy body relax. I saw the psychic wound being closed, lifted up, and out to where it dissolved into the air. It was gone.

Suddenly, I became anxious. Did I really just see that? Did that really just happen? Of course, I had to test it to make sure. Since she was face down on the table and couldn't see me, I slowly started to ease my hands down to her back. When I was about an inch away from her skin, she started to squirm. I rose up a few inches, continuing to channel more healing energy. After another minute passed, I lowered my hands to right above her left lower back. Holding my breath, I gently placed my hands on her skin. Nothing happened. I opened my eyes, my hands on her skin, and still she was not moving.

"Is everything okay?" I asked her to make sure she was alive and had not died of a heart attack at my audacity.

"I am perfectly fine. By the way, are you touching me?"

"Why yes ma'am, I am."

We both couldn't believe it. I spent the rest of the session running my hands over the area increasing and decreasing the pressure because she wanted to make sure that it was gone.

"You mean to tell me that for decades I have suffered with this pain, and in two minutes or less you took it away?"

My inner ego answered, "Yes, that is exactly what I am telling you."

She was in the middle of packing to move to another state, but she returned a week later. She wanted to have a massage to make sure the pain was no longer there. I gave her a complete massage with deep pressure; she did not even feel a thing. She was healed. In my mind I healed her.

This is one of the many examples of spontaneous healing that occurred in my presence. People come in with headaches that disappeared during the session. Some sensitive empaths get close to me and start to cry because they feel so wonderful in my energy. Some people have an automatic opening of their third eye from standing in proximity to me.

All these things started to get to me as my psychic abilities started to grow too. I became unbearable to my friends.

Jenny is one of my oldest and dearest friends and one of the cofounders of the Lotus Petals. She is a healer and one of the most beautiful and humble people I know. She tried many times to tell me to calm down the ego. I completely bashed her for trying to dim my shine. At one point, I even felt like Jenny was jealous because I was having so much accuracy while she was struggling. Talk about a clear mirror right in front of me.

During that time, the Reiki Masters Deceased and the powers that be decided no more would be shared with me. Soon after my last fight with Jenny, my abilities were stopped or were taken away. Whenever a client came before me, I went blank. I saw nothing and felt nothing.

My clients noticed the change in the sessions. "You don't feel present Uma."

I became depressed and angry. This was a cruel joke to play on a humble healer who only wanted to share her gifts with the world.

Funny how quickly we are humbled in the face of adversity. I was no longer the healer. I would tell my students and clients I was only a vessel as I hung my head in self-pity. But even the song and dance of accepting that lowly task didn't bring my powers back. It wasn't until I completely made peace with making a complete and utter fool of myself and asked forgiveness of all those I hurt, that the healing began. When it was restored, I was truly humbled to do the work I do. Ego was released, and I have accepted my role as a vessel.

Ego is a big part of the life lessons here on earth. A lot of books discuss getting rid of the ego once and for all, but that's not necessary. Ego is a necessary part of maintaining human survival. As a spiritual being, we don't know how to survive in this world. We need our ego to help us navigate through experiences.

My suggestion is to make peace with who you are. When you catch yourself making an egotistical ass of yourself, apologize to those you hurt and forgive yourself. Realize that you're a work in progress. Try not to get mad or disillusioned. Elevating the spirit above ego takes time. Depending on how attached you were to your ego; it may take even longer.

Even now, I catch myself in self-dialogue about how I am something extraordinary. I quickly stop, change the conversation, and bring the focus back to the person I am talking to. When this happens, I forgive myself and move on. As a friend of mine says, "Keep it moving."

If you find you're struggling with ego, forgive yourself. Realize there is a reason you are experiencing this. It does feel good to be awakened. It feels good to be conscious of your actions and responsible for your decisions. You feel like an adult for the second time in life.

When good feelings meet natural earthly behavior, a common reaction is to look down on those who haven't grasped the concept like you or who need your help. Just remember, you were once there. The last thing you needed at that point in your journey was for someone to make fun of you or put you down.

When you feel your ego rising, give thanks that you have done good work and made progress for it to rise in the first place. Then with a breath, let the feeling pass and keep it moving!

REFLECT AND JOURNAL

1) Write on a separate piece of paper about three experiences when your ego got in the way of important relationships. Burn them paper in a safe place. As it burns, forgive yourself and release the attachment to those moments. What did you learn that you could take with you as you keep it moving?

_____

_____

_____

_____

_____

_____

_____

_____

_____

_____

_____

_____

_____

_____

_____

CHAPTER 8
BOUNDARIES

When you make a career out of helping people, your boundaries automatically disappear. The following are reasons why that I believe this happens:

1) Since you are in the business of "caring," people assume they can ask you anytime for healing, counseling, readings, messages, or other services because – this *is* what you do right?
2) *You* know you are in the business of "caring." *You* feel you should offer healing, counseling, readings, messages, or other services anytime it is asked of you.
3) Everyone – including you – assumes you *are on* all the time and therefore should be helping automatic. It is in your blood, your "responsibility", and somehow you must honor that divine infusion.

In the beginning of my career, I was a martyr. I took clients as late as 9 p.m. on a school night. I jam-packed my schedule with as much as six clients in one day – my personal limit is three, and if I feel it is really needed, I can extend up to four. On those packed days, I would finish one client, then hurry through lunch while in a phone counseling session with a different client, before a another client came. It didn't stop, and eventually, as expected, I burnt out.

Another big blunder I made in the beginning was to say "yes" to every question or request ever asked. The worst part is, I did it even if my intuition was telling me "no".

A religious male client used to come to once a month for appointments. In the beginning, I gave no information about my psychic abilities. As the months wore on, we became friendly enough to talk during sessions. He would confide about his love relationship issues while I listened and offered my viewpoint.

Once he learned about my psychic abilities, he started to ask questions about his future. I obliged. I accurately predicted many things in his life, and he seemed pleased about everything except my views on his relationship. I told him the relationship he was in wasn't for him, and in fact, I saw another person that was better suited for him.

After awhile, he cancelled his appointments with me because he was moving out of the state for work. When he came for his last session, as a gratitude and goodbye present, I gave him a good reading with his session. I told him that he was going to find work in a matter of months where he was moving. Spirit wanted him to settle in and relax before finding work. During that time, he would meet this girl that would be a long-term companion.

He listened attentively at first, before starting to ask in-depth questions about the girl. What did she look like? When exactly would he meet her? Was she a Christian? I was prepared to answer all those questions, but my guides stopped me. I didn't understand why; however, I chose to listen to my guides and I told him that was all I could offer at that time.

It was hard to get him out my office. He kept pushing me to tell him more information. Smiling, I stayed quiet, before finally telling him he had to leave because I had another client coming. He left, and later that day, I received an email from him. He explained that he didn't mean to offend me by his questions. He explained that the Bible taught him to question psychics in order to weed out the fake from the real ones. That is why he was asking so many questions.

Essentially, he believed he was doing me a favor to prove I was real. It made me glad I listened to my guidance and stopped answering him. If I didn't, when would the questioning stop? Whatever answer I provided would never be good enough because he was coming from a place of doubt, needing proof, instead of a place of acceptance and gratitude.

When I wrote him back to let him know that he didn't offend me. I explained that I would have had to take stock in his opinion for that to happen. Then I apologized for not providing more information, adding that I must be fake then! I wished him well on his trip and ended the correspondence.

I could have reminded him of all the times I provided accurate information. I could have shared the personal stories of miracles and success with other clients. But what would have been the point? People see only what they want to see; that's the beauty of the mind and creating the world we live in.

After that interaction, I developed more resolve when dealing with clients and friends. Generally, people don't come right out to ask me to read them. What I get is a retelling of stories or dreams before the person sits back and waits was if that's my cue to jump in and offer insights. Now I say, "You know that sounds very interesting. If you ever want me to take a look at that psychically, please set up an appointment with me sometime."

With my close friends and inner circle, I am much more relaxed about it. If you have a close friend who owns a mechanic shop, you expect a discount! I do offer my gifts freely with my friends, especially when I know they are not fishing for free sessions, but are truly in the middle of something and need some guidance.

There are acquaintances that fish often. I remain polite and change the topic quickly or let them know I will pray for them to gain an answer for their situation soon.

The biggest misconception about being a healer is that you have your psychic third eye and extrasensory healing open all the time. I really don't know how the Long Island Medium, Theresa does it. I would be stark raving mad at this point if I went around opened all the time and reading everyone.

Spirits do pop in from time to time. It is a surprise to see them show up behind someone. Usually, I acknowledge them and keep it moving. In order to commutate with them, I would need to tune in. I tend not to do that unless there is urgency or need for the communication to happen.

As a highly sensitive empath, I can easily become a psychic sponge, soaking in all the vibes from other people and beings. Once I was working with a sad and depressed client that came in for a reading about her breakup with her boyfriend. After the session, I forgot to wash my hands. I was hurrying to get upstairs to get my kids down to bed.

After my kids were in bed, I felt so depressed and sad that I was single. I felt like my life was nothing because I didn't have a man. I proceeded to eat a pint of Häagen-Dazs coffee ice cream (my drug of choice) and wash it down with a glass of wine! I then dragged my sorry self to bed, all alone and nothing.

When I woke up in the morning, I had a splitting headache. I asked my guides what in the heck was going on? They showed me the situation where I walked my client out the door and closed up the studio. They pointed out the bathroom where I usually washed my hands. I realized I didn't break from the client. That's when I began to laugh. I'm inherently fine being in a relationship or being single. I don't get caught up with the need for another person to make my life whole. The reflection of my tendency versus my empathetic experience with this client generated a lot of compassion. I realized that the emotional state I had experienced was this woman's feeling on a daily basis. I immediately sent her healing and prayed for her to love herself and learn to take care of her own needs.

You have seen my list, now here are manifestations I believe occur when awakened ones do not establish boundaries. When people don't have a clear set of boundaries, they tend to encourage certain things.

There is an unconscious resonance released to the world that your time is not valuable. What is really communicated is that your life is not valuable because other people's demands are more important than your own. The universe will listen and abide, making that unconscious thought a reality. What starts to happen is that fun plans start to fall apart. That date you were really looking forward to is suddenly cancelled. That vacation you really wanted to take will be out of reach due to financial difficulty. The things *you* want will move further and further away. The things people want from you will move to the forefront. Your system becomes drained of energy and resources.

The physical body and mind are organisms that work in partnership with your Spirit to make up your vessel. When you do not eat properly (because you are rushing), you do not sleep enough (because you are working), and you do not take time out to relax the mind (because of obsessing), your entire organism will suffer.

Boundaries are extremely important to set in your personal life as well. It does no good to be firm in your boundaries at work and then leave your social circles wide opened for behaviors you do not need in your life.

I was a Jersey Girl when I went to college for my Bachelors and Master's Degrees. If it's one thing I learned from New Jersey, despite the awesome hair, stylish clothes, and street attitude, it was how to curse. My best friend Christie was a born and bred Italian Jerseyan. Every word out her mouth, at that time (because Christie is now a mature and wonderful woman), was a curse word. She came up came up new and colorful ways to curse. I picked the habit up. Soon we were two happy, pretty girls that cursed like drunken sailors.

I had the habit of cursing up until very recently. While the cursing was not as colorful or frequent as my Jersey Girl days, I occasionally dropped a well-placed f-bomb.

I once dated, before becoming friends with, a very likable guy. He was such a character; I immensely enjoyed our daily talks. However, when started to grow spiritually, I reached a vibration where words became golden and instrumental in my manifestations.

I became very careful how I used my words and began to notice that what I said manifested almost instantaneously in my life. My tolerance for harsh language or critical words dropped significantly. They would actually hurt my ears so much that I had to hold my hands over my ears whenever someone cursed or said negative or unkind to others or themselves.

When this started, I knew almost instantly that my friendship with this guy was going to either change or end. I started by asking him to stop cursing around me. At first, he obliged. The habit was so ingrained in him that he always slipped back in to it. My approach became firmer. Every time he uttered a curse word, I would say, "Please don't curse."

After awhile, he got mad angry and felt I was being hypocritical. He pointed out how I used to curse more than he did. It broke my heart to let him go, but I had to for my own sake. He was not ready to change, and really shouldn't have to if he didn't want to. It was a boundary I needed to created and hold firm to respect that line.

The biggest issue I see people have in making boundaries is concern about how other people will think or respond. If you have been one way your entire life, then suddenly change, there is fear about appearing fake be called out by your inner circle.

Beloved, let me tell you now, if those around you do not support you with your life changing decisions, then they are not the ones to consider for your inner circle.

I have come to my best friends with wild requests over the years, and no one ever put me down or doubted me. I have changed my religious paths, my food preferences, and even my name several times. Each time, my best friends have supported me with love. This is what you need and deserve in your life.

Living with strong boundaries gives you permission to be who you want to be without asking permission from someone else. That is essentially what you are doing when you cower before the opinions or actions of others; you're asking their permission to live your life.

Set your boundaries in place and stand firm with them. Take relief in the idea that it may be a boundary set for life or a boundary set for the present time only. I had a friend who became celibate for two years because she needed to explore time alone. We respected her space and never judged or criticized her. When she came out of that lesson to start dating again, we supported her then as well.

Of all the chapters written so far, this is *by far* the most precious gift I can offer. Please, set your boundaries and have faith that those who are special in your life will respect them. Believe that those who do not care you honor your boundaries, will disappear from your life. Either way, it is a win-win scenario because you get to grow spiritually and take those that matter along with you for the ride.

1) Make a set schedule for your work hours and stick to it. Only make allowances outside of your schedule if your intuition dictates it is okay and not your ego. How did this change your week?

_____

_____

_____

_____

_____

2) Make a list of boundaries that you can instill in your personal life. What will you do if someone crosses your boundary?

_____

_____

_____

_____

_____

CHAPTER 9
BECOMING AUTHENTIC

Authenticity is a reoccurring theme in this book. The need to be authentic in your relationships and outlook on life is vital to awakening. Let's explore on a deeper level what it means to be authentic.

I receive messages from Spirit at the start of every year about where I should focus in my evolving path. In 2010, I learned there was a need for spiritual community — Sangha — to help foster my growth. I took the message seriously and joined the plethora of spiritual groups in my area on Meetup.com. Usually the messages come the beginning of the New Year, but that particular message came at the end of 2009. It moved me so much, I not only joined other groups, but created the Manassas Reiki, Yoga & Meditation group.

In 2011, my spirit-based message was fine-tuning from group relationships to more one-on-one spiritual partnerships. I started to let go of unhealthy relationships with some friends and family members and invite in healthier ones. There is a note of caution here; when we discuss unhealthy relationships, it isn't always referring to the other person being negative. Sometimes we have to leave relationships because the people love us so much, they enable us in our unhealthy behavior. It isn't always the other person that is unhealthy; it can be us too.

In 2012, the message was to live an authentic life. Now, the funny thing is how synchronicity works when you are tapped in and following the Universe's command. I received an essential oil massage from a lovely healer in my area. As we were talking during the session, I realized we both were given the message to live more authentic lives. We were amazed that we heard the same call, but not too surprised. Synchronicity tends to line up the more and more you follow your path.

So what does it mean to be authentic? It means to do things that feel right to *you*. This can be a big jump for many who are auto-tuned to listen to the voices of those who have gone before us. From childhood, we are taught what is required to be considered a good citizen in the home, school, community, and public arena. It can feel safer to listen to others. It can also be considered a time saver to avoid experiencing the pain and trauma of learning your own lessons. You build off of other people's experiences, modeling your action based on what they've learned.

"I told you so," is the mantra evoked when we decide to do our own thing and perhaps fail at what we tried. Usually, we stop once the mantra is in full effect. But I tell you, dear readers, do not cower and definitely do not stop.

We came to this life to be observers. We came to experience and learn through play. No one can fully understand how bad an idea it is to date someone known as a "bad boy" until you experience it for yourself. No matter how much personal experience is conveyed from someone else, it doesn't communicated the pain and frustration that comes from actually experiencing the situation yourself. No amount of fair warning or statistical reports convey how disgusting you feel after a night out with friends and you overdo it the partying and/or drinking. You definitely need at least one hangover morning to understand that concept!

Awakening is a journey of self-discovery and learning. You test and learn what you want and what works for you. For some people, they need to be in the earth school learning longer than others. It's like real school — you have straight-A students and those basically skidding by. No matter what, we all graduate *unless* you choose to leave school early (by taking your life), but that is a whole other chapter... or book for that matter.

Don't make awakening a competition. Don't aim to be the A student. It really doesn't matter. Who is grading you exactly? If you answer your peers, then your ego is in charge and it may be a good idea to return to your studies. Ego 101 may be a good refresher course.

As you don't make this a race, try to hurry through experiences to "win" at something. It's also required to not judge others on their journey. If an A student notices another student struggling, leave them be. Neither offer to help them (it's not your place) or make fun of them. We've all been there. None of us like it when someone else offers condescending help or makes fun of us.

Being authentic means living your life the way you want to with no apologies. If you like to play drums, play them. If you like to bring incense with you everywhere, go for it. If you like to pray over your meals in public areas, do so proudly. No matter what calling you have, do it with pride. You are a unique individual. Despite popular thought, an awakening *is* all about you.

I have a monthly metaphysical book club that meets once a month at Barnes and Noble bookstore to focus on books based on spiritual topics. In my month to choose a book, I suggested, *The Purpose Driven Life* by Rick Warren.

This book sat in my library for years, but I hadn't read it. I heard it was one of the bestselling books in the world, and knew a little about the pastor/author, so I thought it would be a good suggestion for our book club. Boy, was I wrong.

I struggled to read this book, which this was a first because I'm a bookworm that can finish multiple books a week. I devour books, since reading is one of my favorite hobbies. The book came with me as a travel companion to the weekend seminar I previously mentioned at Edgar Cayce's A.R.E. in Virginia Beach. The psychic development and classes were twelve hours long. I will never forget that first night as I lay in bed, too tired to talk on the phone, but not tired enough to go to sleep. I decided to read the book.

That's when I came to the chapter where the author discusses how life is not about *you* it is about *God*. I had to stop. This went against everything I believed. I knew I couldn't be authentic and continue reading a book that completely went against my path.

Fear did rise up in me. What would people think? This book was my suggestion for the book club. What if I didn't attend the meeting for the book I chose? I battled with the idea. As it weighed heavily on my mind, I talked to one of my girlfriends about it. She was also having a hard time reading it and was deciding whether or not to push through or trash it.

During the seminar, one of the speakers asked about how we make difficult decisions in life and how we decide what to do. I raised my hand and brought up the book ordeal. I was stuck; if I was to remain authentic, I would have to cancel the book reading. I felt like that would be letting people down. The speaker smiled, sharing how she had a hard time reading it herself. The experience brought up feelings of insecurity for her as well, being that it was a worldwide bestselling book. Message received.

When we live authentically, we often choose to make decisions that go against the majority of the crowd. We make choices based on what works best for us at that moment, not what's popular opinion.

When you decide to live authentically, you have to put aside what other people will think about you. Faith is necessary to stand firm in belief that that the right people will support and stand by you no matter what. Then even if there is no one to hold your hand, be resolved to take comfort in the words my mom always use to say, "You come into this world alone, and you leave alone." This life is not about accommodating others; it's about living *your truth*.

REFLECT AND JOURNAL

1) What are three things you strongly believe in but keep to yourself? Write them down.

_____

_____

_____

_____

_____

2) Make a commitment to share these three things with three different people. Gauge their reactions and your response. How did you feel before, during, and after?

_____

_____

_____

_____

_____

CHAPTER 10
SUPERNATURAL PHENOMENA

Though this was briefly touched on in previous chapters, supernatural phenomena is a topic we cannot ignore. Many may read this feeling that they don't have, or do even believe in, psychic gifts. Even if people don't understand or believe in supernatural phenomena, it doesn't change the fact that they exist. I'm living proof that it does.

When I first awakened, I became more mindful and grateful for this life I lived. I became less ego-minded and more spirit-led. Peace pervaded my life, and my friends and family noticed the shift right away. Years of anger and hurt seemed to dissipate almost instantaneously. I was happy and content.

My psychic senses started opening up after that shift. I would massage people like I normally did, but then I would get visions of my clients doing random things or hear messages for them. At first, I ignored it, thinking my mind was just wandering. Then the messages and visions got clearer. I knew I had to start telling the target of the visions what I was seeing.

For instance, while I was massaging a woman, I clearly saw her and her husband eating lunch outside where they were sitting at a table under an umbrella. I couldn't hear what they were talking about, but I could see that they were arguing, and I knew it was about money. Inside I heard not to worry, things would end up going smoothly. Walking by faith, I told her exactly what I saw. She was surprised and confirmed the scenario happened exactly that way the day before. The message relaxed her, providing comfort in knowing that even though the situation wasn't solved, it would work out eventually.

The Clair Senses are gifts that each person has embedded within our energy system. Some of us are very good at one Clair Sense over another, while some are multi-talented. The truth is, we each have a Clair gift that we can call on when we need help or to make decisions.

I believe the Clairs are given to provide healing and advice when we need it. They're also given for us to help others. The Clair gifts really show how we aren't alone and we are not having separate life experiences. They open the awareness to experience how we're all dependent on each other for survival. For these reasons, when you have a psychic sense opening up, do not shut it down.

Many of my students had innate psychic abilities as children. Out of fear of the experiences or repression from outside sources, they shut the abilities down. When they reached their 30s-40s, many found that their gifts return, even if fear was still there.

My advice to anyone living on Fear Street about Clair Senses is to get over it. You are given a gift for a reason; you are meant to use it. Many of my clients pay me to do intuitive readings. It is such a waste of money. They're highly intuitive and psychically inclined, yet they turn to me for answers to questions even though they are wired to answer for themselves.

While awakening, you may or may not have personal brushes with the Clairs. For both audiences, it is a good idea to have an understanding of what Clair Sense are. Even if they don't apply to you, it is important to understand more about the other gifts people on the awakened path flow in.

Most psychic abilities are grouped into five categories — the Clairs. These are "other" senses that open as you become awakened. They are used in conjunction with your regular five senses (vision, hearing, touch, smell and taste) to make you a complete sensory being.

Clairvoyance

This is one of the most popular gifts, since it is the most common ability used by psychics and fortune tellers. Clairvoyance is the gift of sight — and no it does not pertain to eyesight. It refers to the third eye visions that give you glimpses into the past, present, and future. These visions can be prophetic where they tell of events yet to happen or can be historical where they relay information from a past event. Some visions can tell what is happening here and now to provide insight into a situation that is occurring.

When you first start being clairvoyant, you may not be adapt at determining the timing of the vision, whether it is past, present, or future. That is because time and space are constructs of the mind. Einstein proved the constructs of space and time do not exist. This is why we can "see" events in people's lives.

For me, the sight appears as a running clip from a movie screen where I see people and actions around them. As this gift developed more, I began to distinguish if it had happened, was happening, about to happen, or was going to happen. You will also be able to distinguish time clearly as you progress.

Clairaudience

The clairaudient are mostly identified as mediums or seers who "hear" messages with their psychic ears. They hear a voice in their mind that is different from their own small, inner voice. This separate voice speaks to them, revealing what is happening in a situation. The origin of the voice can come from a myriad of places, including spirit guides, guardian angels, guides or angels of the person being read, deceased relatives and loved ones, or even the voice of an issue.

I once read a woman who had experienced so many difficult times that they banded together to become a voice. Whenever she tried to do something new, this voice would put her down or tell her not to do it. She had given a voice to her fears, allowing them to grow in intensity every time she listened to them. That weakened her inner voice of intuition.

Telepathy is a form of clairaudience where you can communicate with the living through inner dialogue. Most people recognize this gift when they think of someone and soon after that person calls. The fun part is trying to figure out who sent the message first! Did you think of the person and they called or was the person thinking of you and decided to call?

The majority of time, the voice can be heard within your head; however, sometimes it can be heard with actual physical hearing. Sometimes I hear someone call my name or give a warning when there is no one in sight. In time, you can develop this gift to distinguish the source of what you're hearing, whether it's your own intuition, insight from a spirit guide, or a deceased relative trying to help in situations for your client.

Clairsentience

Most healers and empaths use the clairsentient ability. This is the gift of feeling. It's the ability to understand and process what someone else is going through on an emotional and mental level. This happens naturally when you're close to the person. If your girlfriend is undergoing a divorce from her husband of thirty years and is feeling devastated, you will feel awful also. Even though the situation isn't physically happening to you, in the metaphysical world, it is happening on a sensory level.

When close connections are formed with people, we invite them to be part of our spider web. That's why it's important, as we discussed in previous chapters, to choose your company carefully. When you make an agreement to let others into your web, you can feel and experience what they go through if you have a strong clairsentient gift. This is why I fill my web with happy, positive, and joyous people!

Medical intuitives also fall under this category. They are able to ascertain a person's conditions by sometimes seeing it, but they most often feel it. Many times, before I even touch a client, I start to feel an ache in my upper back or knee or hip area. Then when the client is on my massage table, I am able to go right to the location of the pain. It surprises them every time that happens.

People in this category have to be very careful not to become a psychic sponge. They so closely align to someone's situation or energy that they start to take on the attributes of that energy. Many times, I see this cause a lot of healers to get sick or depressed. They're worn out or drained because they forgot to break off the connection after working with a client. It has happened to me too!

A client once came for an intuitive reading; she was filled with sadness and depression. Her reading revealed she was on the cusp of ending a relationship with her live-in boyfriend of ten years. Like I mentioned earlier, after she left, I forgot to wash my hands in order to break the connection. That led to a night of ingesting double dinners, a pint of ice cream, and drank a half bottle of wine.

When I woke up in the morning with the sugar, alcohol, and self-pity hangover, I asked for guidance. I was shown how I forgot to break from the client and carried her feelings with me. I think I double wash now because of that incident.

Clairgustance

This is one of the least discussed gifts because very few people have it or it appears sporadically. This gift includes a psychic sense of smell. I have only experienced it a few times. Usually it happens when I am in mediumship mode and a spirit enters the room. I once had a person on the phone and his sister was in a coma. As we were working to try to contact her, I started to smell cigarette smoke in my room. I don't smoke. No one else smokes in my house. I asked my client if his sister smoked. He answered, "Oh yes, like a pack a day!"

Many times angels appear around us with what smells like a ripe bouquet of flowers. It's very similar to the perfume a lot of grandmother's from the 40's to 60's used. The smell can be very sweet and flowery. People tend to experience this smell when they are getting in a car. If you do, I would caution you to drive carefully and pay attention. If your assigned angel is showing up, they are very intent on keeping you safe in that particular situation.

Claircognizance

Clear-knowing is my most dominant gift. This sense of knowing is the gift of successful counselors, psychics, seers, and intuitives.

Have you ever had a friend ask you a question and you answered in such a profound and helpful way that you took note of it?

When we let go of the need to control everything, we become open and accepting of the universal flow. That is when we become a conduit, putting ego aside to let Spirit stream through.

Many times I've helped clients and friends in personal situations and find the messages coming through for them can also apply to situations in my life. Spirit is excellent at multitasking like that! When you think about it, we are all here to help each other. It naturally occurs for there to be an attraction to two people who are going through the same thing at the same time. Not only is it easier to intuit because the feeling is fresh, it is a way you both can share your experiences and learn to grow from it together.

Becoming awakened tunes you I to the universal flow. You begin to develop senses for survival that include the Clairs. Many times people feel they need to make a business out of it these psychic gives, but that's not the case for everyone. Check with your intuition to find out what you're supposed to do with your abilities. Sometimes your gifts develop sufficiently for you to navigate your path. Sometimes they open wider for you to become a beacon that helps a multitude of people on their path. Neither is better; it is a matter of the purpose or calling a person has in their life.

1) After learning about each of the Clair Senses, which one best identifies you?

_____

_____

_____

_____

_____

2) What activities can you do to enhance your most predominant Clair?

_____

_____

_____

_____

_____

CHAPTER 11
GRATITUDE

All the Clair skills are blessings; while they can be developed, they cannot be forced. Many times I come across avid meditators and enlightened folk who demand to know my personal spiritual discipline.

They want answers as to why I can do my work and they cannot. I don't have an answer for them. I really don't know why. I have always chalked it up to several reasons, including a blessing and a grace bestowed on me at birth that later bloomed in my thirties.

Another reason could also be my many past lives as a healer. When you do something continuously in many lifetimes, it helps it become second nature for you in this lifetime. Think of the many gifted children who never heard classical music, but they play like expert pianists the first time they try. They were not taught, they *knew*.

Another reason can be the path of Bhakti, which I unconsciously follow. When I lived at the ashram in 2010, I learned there were four paths of Yoga that can guide a person to achieve enlightenment:

Karma Yoga – The Yoga of Action

This path is for the more outgoing people who like to socialize and involve community in their spiritual work. It is the path of volunteering that involves selfless service and putting away the ego for the good of all.

Raja Yoga – The Yoga of Physical and Mental Control

Also called Royal Yoga, this focuses completely on the self and becoming aware of how different ways of thinking shift the consciousness from materialistic to spiritual needs. I like to think that this path is more for the introverts who like to work in solitude with themselves and God.

Jnana Yoga – The Yoga of Knowledge and Wisdom

This is considered the most difficult path. It involves self-inquiry and determined willpower to break the idea that God is separate in order to live in the idea of oneness where He resides within us. Many enlightened people choose this path because it is very powerful and enlightening for the seeker.

Bhakti Yoga – The Path of Devotion or Divine Love

In this emotional path, the seeker is motivated by the love – love of of God and love of everything around them. The seeker surrenders completely to God and usually practices chanting, singing, dancing and channeling God for the greatest good.

As with all things that have happened in my life, I did not seek Bhakti Yoga. It sought me. When I was a stay-at-home mother and wife, my only duties were to take care of my children, husband, and home.

I did not have any interest in being awakened or enlightened. There definitely wasn't an interest in being spiritual. I was content. I remember one day; I put my babies down for their afternoon nap. While I was mopping the kitchen, I was giving thanks in my mind —a regular custom for me — expressing gratitude for everything.

"God, thank you for giving me this beautiful kitchen in my own home. Thank you for giving me a floor to mop. Thank you for giving me enough money to buy a mop!"

I know it sounds silly, but that was my mindset. I was grateful and content. In my gratitude and happiness, my Spirit grew. My awakening happened shortly after this time. I definitely believe when you live a life of gratitude, it creates the fast track to enlightenment.

When I finally joined the path of awakening, I decided to follow the Yogic route because it was open and accepting of all races, classes, cultures, and religious groups. The open and accepting policy attracted me.

For a long time, I struggled with being a good spiritual student. Once I entered the Yoga Path, I felt I had to become vegetarian, meditate, and do yoga daily. I was sure I shouldn't drink, have a multitude of love relationships, or fun nights out. I felt that my awakening, my psychic gifts, and wisdom all were dependent on healthy habits. If I did not follow one, the other would fail.

I struggled in vain to keep up with the other super healthy spiritual people, but I just couldn't cut it. I love life, fun, and adventure. I felt betrayed by the Universe for making me choose between enjoyment and spirit. It really felt like I was being selfish if I chose to have a life I really enjoyed living.

As you probably know by now, this is when the Universe lines up synchronistic events to help and provide the answers needed.

It was a regular day at the ashram where we were in Yoga theory class, learning about the four paths of Yoga. I remember feeling dejected because, as with all spiritual disciplines, a lot of physical and mental requirements were expected to achieve enlightenment.

When the teacher reached the path of Bhakti Yoga, he pointed me out and said, "Uma is able to do the things she does because she is in love with God and has completely surrendered her life to God."

I flushed in response. I did love God; I always have. From the tender age of nine when I wanted to grow up and become a nun, to choosing a college run by nuns, to seeking out a religious route to show devotion to Him. If it's one thing I can say with certainty, it's that I love God.

The idea that there is a path to God based solely on devotion and love made so much sense to me. This was my path. It was full of emotion and love — everything I followed.

If you are not yet awakened, here is a reminder — everything starts with being grateful. Instead of looking to where you want to be and what you want to accomplish, be grateful for what you already have.

Back in 2014 I attended an Intenders Circle at a friend's house every Monday night. We would meet, share food, talk, laugh, and then get really serious during our weekly meeting.

As we went around the circle, we each had to list our intentions for what we wanted to manifest in our lives. No request was too big or small; everything in between was encouraged, and supported, by this group.

What's interesting about this is that we each had to start by listing things we were grateful for. We gave thanks for what we had already received to show the Universe that we were mindful and appreciative. This opens the door for more blessings to follow through!

When the Universe speaks, it will share messages redundantly until you get it. Any path you choose to reach enlightenment and your awakening is fine. You decide what is best for *you*.

It really doesn't matter what path you choose. In the end, the path chooses you. If you can just surrender the reins a little bit, loosen the control and your mindset of what things should be like or how you should be, I find much growth will come your way as a thank you from the Universe. Just make sure to stay grateful for everything you have.

REFLECT AND JOURNAL

1) Which of the four Yoga Paths would you choose to follow? Why?

_____

_____

_____

_____

_____

2) Make a list of ten things you are grateful for right now in your life. Repeat these things every night before you go to bed. Journal the changes that occur in your life after those ten days are complete.

_____

_____

_____

_____

_____

CHAPTER 12
PROGRESS AND SELF-HEALING

When I was a new Reiki teacher, I had a stipulation on my classes that students had to wait a minimum of one month before they could take the next level between Reiki I and II. Then they had to wait an additional six months before taking Reiki III. I felt I was doing it for their own good, to make them slow down and enjoy the unfolding, undergo the healing crisis, and take time to line up with their intuitive and psychic abilities.

I thought I had Spirit's blessing on this move. As a result of my decision, I started to lose students to other teachers who didn't have those demands and were offering classes in a quicker time frame. When I finally meditated on this, it was revealed that I was slowing down progress of some students in a hope to save the few who were racing ahead. I was reminded that while the majority of us do not do our own inner work, there are many out there who do. I shouldn't punish the workers because of the few that needed to slow down. Spirit reminded me that time will teach them lessons. While it will come in a more harsh way, it is what is needed for those particular people.

There was one client who came to see me for an intuitive reading. She was a regular at my studio who had been coming to classes. I hadn't seen very much in a year. I knew she had started her own business. I guessed she was too busy to come for events. When she arrived after the absence, I was shocked. She looked pale and weary. I knew something was wrong on a deep level. We quickly started her session because the messages were coming in rapidly.

When we began, I was told that there were disconnects between her Spirit and ego-self. It was in her cards to be a healer and open a business. However, she jumped the gun and rented a space for a year, investing money in her business without grasping what her gifts actually were. She didn't know exactly what she was bringing to offer to the world. As a result, her business failed and she had no clients. Not only that, her love relationship was failing. She was deeply depressed.

I told her that it was the time to work on herself and uncover the emotions she had hidden for so long. Once she figured that out, the lessons would be learned and released. Then her life as a healer would resume.

She was upset. This would mean a big financial loss for her. I told her that sometimes we have to undergo harsh life lessons to learn things. She was adamant that her intuition was working. In addition, I and another healer gave her the message to go ahead with her plans. It took a long time to sort it out, but eventually she understood that she was seeing what she wanted to see.

You can receive ten different psychic readings that each tell you the same thing. The one thing they cannot tell you is timing. Time and space are constructs of the mind. When we do a psychic reading, we are outside the realm of the mind. We are now in the realm of spirit. Myself and the other healer picked up that she was a healer and could be a successful healer in business. First, she needed to learn to listen carefully to her inner voice and to trust the process to unfold. Spirit is not going to entrust someone else's energy into your hands if you still need to be worked on and healed of your own issues. Now I am not saying that all awakened people are perfect beings. Far from it. Being awakened sounds like more than it really is. All it really comes down to is that you have an awareness that life is sacred and you start to take the steps to honor and acknowledging that life within others.

An awakening in your life does not mean you will appear or function at your finest. It may take months or years to even get to an appearance of your finest. An awakening has more to do with a change in the way you perceive the world.

I find the most successful awakened people have made peace with many emotional and social issues in their lives. To work on physical characteristics is the last process. That is more crucial because it comes with investigating and understanding your life mentally, emotionally, and spiritually.

I find having a daily practice that includes self-healing is crucial. Think about it, you can go to a healer to get work done weekly or you can work on yourself daily.

When you do your self-healing, you learn insights about your behavior. You learn to release old thoughts and patterns that no longer serve you. Also, you become more aware of how your habits affect your energy. Then you learn how to create new behaviors to foster your growth.

I find the first thing that stops when we get busy with life are our personal healing practice. There is a beautiful Buddhist quote that says, "Meditate for twenty minutes a day. If you are too busy, then meditate for an hour a day."

We must begin to integrate with the understanding that if we do not settle peace into our minds and beings, we do not settle peace into our work. Once we fully integrate this concept into our life, we cannot imagine beginning anything without first centering yourself.

As with everything, practice makes perfect. When I first started with my morning routine, I did fifteen minutes of yoga, ten minutes of meditation, and five minutes of journal writing for a complete half of an hour of spiritual practice.

Over time, my intuition led me to extend the time to up to a half hour of meditation, half hour of yoga, and fifteen minutes of journal writing. This never stayed constant.

Some days, when things were heavy on my mind, I would stay in my sanctuary for two hours because I had to mentally sort things out. Some mornings, I was in the right groove, and after my meditation, I headed out the door. You really learn to play it by ear in order to figure out what you need at that time for you to thrive.

Personal practice differs from person to person. I have an atheist friend who does not believe in half the things I do, but he still has his personal practice every day. He gets up and works out at the same time every morning because it sets the intent for his day. For some other people, getting up and drinking a cup of coffee while sitting on their back porch puts them in a contemplative mood, which is close to a meditative state.

The idea is that as an awakened individual, you are constantly receiving messages meant to enhance your soul growth. You need to set aside some time to reflect on these truths and apply them to your life.

Healing is required because as you grow spiritually, you will be releasing old thought patterns and behaviors that no longer serve you. You need to be at a higher energy to accept the new ones coming in to make your life purposeful.

1) Do you have a morning practice? If so, what is it? If not, what would you add to make a morning practice?

_____

_____

_____

_____

_____

_____

_____

_____

_____

_____

FINAL NOTE

I have been teaching these concepts for many years and the time came to publish because frankly my students and clients pushed me to do it!

While I understand that many of the beliefs I hold have helped many on their individual paths, I am well aware this book is not for everyone and may cause some confusion in your life. It may go against beliefs you have held for a long time, or against beliefs of your family, society or religious group. I mean no harm.

I simply wish to share what I have learned on my own Path. Because it has brought much success, happiness, joy, love, peace and contentment for me, I wish to share it with you.

Stay in touch as I look forward to hearing what your thoughts are on this book. If after reading, you would like to book me for a consultation I can most certainly do that too.

I find we are all awakening at different points in our lives and the process differs in length. There is no need to hurry or slow down, we are all moving at the right speed and we are in the right time. It is imperative for us to be mindful of each other's journey and assist in whatever way we can. This is my contribution to the process. It is my hope, that those of you who are beginning to awaken will find some comfort in reading this book because it will help you understand your journey a little bit more. That and the fact that you are not alone. We are all going through it with you.

In Love and Light Always,
Uma Alexandra Beepat

About the Author

Uma Alexandra Beepat was born in London, England. She spent her childhood years growing up in the Caribbean island of Barbados and South American country of Guyana. She moved to the United States when she was 17 for college. She lived in New Jersey, Philadelphia and West Palm Beach before settling into her home and business in Northern Virginia.

Uma has always been an intuitive and empathic child since birth and with the mentorship of her mother and grandmother, developed her gifts quite naturally. Her mother taught her about the value of dreams as she was a prophetic dreamer and her grandmother taught her the value of natural remedies and following the signs, as she was a seer and a natural folk-medicine woman.

Uma also derived much early talent from her mother's circle of friends including Aunty Paula, Aunty Iris, Aunty Patsy, Aunty Chandra, Aunty Lauren, Aunty Suscil, Aunty Nalini and Aunty Debbie. She watched and learned from these women their highly powerful spiritual and religious beliefs and applied them to her life. These aunts unknowingly fostered the strong, Feminine Divine which is prevalent in Uma's Spirit now and which provides most of the healing capabilities she uses.

In 2008 she was divinely led to massage school as was described in one of the chapters above. In 2009, based off of a dream, she quit her job at a local spa franchise and founded Lotus Wellness Center (www.lotuswellnesscenter.net).

At this time, she was working with the Christ Consciousness due to her Anglican background. Christ the Avatar would appear to her repeatedly and explain certain parables in the bible as he meant them to be understood. She would share these insights with her students. He also explained many metaphysical concepts that she would learn from her students were true and shared by authors in several books.

Uma bases much of her spiritual learning on contact and teachings given to her in meditations and visions, and less on book learning.

In 2010 she was led to Yogaville to complete her yoga training and take initiation under Swami Satchidinanda. Even though Swami had been deceased eight years prior, he came to her in dreams and asked her to attend his school. She complied.

With the work of her Swami on the other side, her psychic and intuitive abilities developed rapidly. She began to journey easily across the worlds and interacts with people both living and departed. She started leaving the work of the Christ consciousness and entering in the realms of the Hindu Goddesses. They took her and her learning to new levels and are the driving force behind this book.

In 2011, a mystic approached Uma and gave her the message that she was meant to heal and teach thousands of people. She was told to go to India and more would be revealed.

In 2012 arrangements were made (spiritually) for her to travel to the mystical countries of India, Peru (Macchu Picchu) and Morocco. Uma received valuable downloads from these trips and a strengthening of her psychic abilities.

It was in India she met a female Guru who firmly established the path of healer and speaker for her. She began to openly share her gifts with the world at this point. The Guru told her that there would be a teacher in her hometown that would take her work to the next level.

Following the Guru's words of advice, Uma was divinely led, contacted and learned under the amazing tutelage of Wanda Lasseter Lundy, a noted psychic healer and Minister in the Northern Virginia area. Wanda too has given her blessing for this book to be released.

Uma's work began to diversify into different avenues. She became the healer and seer in the community and grew her list of modalities to include hypnosis, IET, Bach Flower Remedies, doTERRA oils, Theta Healing, Tuning Fork Therapy, Access Consciousness, Life Coaching and Past Life Regression which she learned directly from Dr. Brian Weiss himself.

In 2016 Uma journeyed to the Arthur Findlay College in Stansted, UK and began her mediumship training. She was offered private mentorship by two of the college tutors and at this time she is still undergoing psychic mediumship training with respected teachers Eileen Davis, Matthew Smith, Colin Bates, John Johnson, John Holland, Janet Nohavec to name a few. Uma is available to host mediumship circles and development training in psychic mediumship.

At this time, Uma is still working and teaching at her studio Lotus Wellness Center (www.lotuswellnesscenter.net) in Manassas, VA and part time at the Spirit University in Sarasota, FL. Uma also travel teaches throughout the US and Europe at centers and studios she is invited to. Uma is a Reiki Master Teacher, Licensed Massage Therapist, Certified Reflexologist, Munay Ki Shamanic Practitioner and Yoga and Ayurveda Instructor among other things.

She offers Intuitive consultations, healing and readings to clients both in Virginia and out of state or country with the help of Skype. She calls them intuitive consultations because she shares information that the client **needs** to know at that given point to help further them on their soul path. She also has the ability to bilocate (split energy) and work with healing energy on the client as she is reading them. This is experienced by the client as tingling in the head, third eye area and feeling warmth or tingling throughout the body.

Uma loves doing the work she does but only second to being a mom. Her two boys Nathan and Joshua are the special joys in her life and they spend an inordinate amount of time having fun! Raising a medium and shamanic healer is fun in of itself!

It is Uma's wish to bring healing, expansion and awareness to as many people as she can before she exits the earth school. She feels she was sent here to specifically connect people back to their true purpose and in doing so, works with the Awakening energy. She also enjoys teaching people on the Art of Suffering, to accept what is and how to make the most of grievous situations.

Stay in Touch!

Blog: https://umalotusflower.blog/
YouTube: Lotus Inspiration1111
Instagram: umalotusflower78
Twitter: lotuswellness1
Facebook: www.facebook.com/umalotusflower/
Linked In: Uma Alexandra Beepat

Printed in the United States
By Bookmasters